Environment

A letter from the Author

Hello,

*Welcome to **Environment**.*
It's a great opportunity to explore our world: the earth, the air and the seas. And, of course, our daily lives in our environment. We ask lots of questions!

We go under the sea to learn about whales. There's a special word for whales, dolphins and porpoises: cetaceans. We can see these animals in Asia, Europe and North and South America. We ask: can humans co-exist with these animals? There is a report on an environmental project in Scotland. This combines research, education – and a beautiful sailing boat. We also discuss energy: can wind farms provide electricity for the future? How can a wind machine in a school be part of this research?

We have to look after our environment when we produce food. How can we do this? Can consumers help workers to get good prices for their food? Read some personal stories and new ideas about this.

How can we discover more about the environment through research, science, and personal actions? Why does nature usually have the last word? Read about natural disasters, and how they affect us, too.

*You can find personal answers to some of these questions in the Environmental Eye. Things to research, to think about, and to do in **your** environment. There are also some great photos.*

Enjoy it!

Susan Holden

contents

TO THE **TOPICS** USERS

VOCABULARY You can find the key vocabulary for every article in the **WORD FILE** on that page. The pictures will also help you to guess the meaning in context. There is a summary of useful vocabulary on the **Check it out** page. Finally, you can use the *Macmillan Essential Dictionary* to consolidate the new vocabulary.

WEBSITES There is a list of useful website addresses on page 2. Remember that websites change. Be selective!

Check it out

Verbs

consume	contaminate	decrease
destroy	increase	kill
lose	pollute	preserve
protect	research	save

Issues

campaign	find out	investigate
photograph	record	research

Water

current	dam	drinking water
fresh water	rain	salt water
shower	tide	waste water
water table	wave	wetland

Air

cloud	storm	wind

Earth

biodiversity	desert	forest
land	soil	vegetation

Agriculture

Nouns

crops	fields	irrigation

Verbs

cultivate	grow	harvest
irrigate	plant	water

Energy

solar energy	wind power

People

emigration	immigration	population growth

Animals

habitat	migration	population

Pollution

acid rain	chemicals	contamination
detergents	fertilizers	industrial waste
pesticides	pollutants	sewage

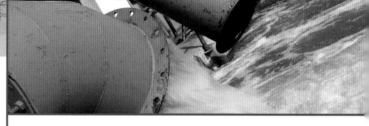

Disasters

earthquake	drought	famine
fire	flood	storm
tornado [hurricane/tropical cyclone/typhoon/whirlwind]		

Environmental issues

ecology	eco-system	eco-tourism
global warming		sustainable development

Sources and Resources

We consulted a lot of sources for 'Environment': people, books and the Internet. If you want to find out more about any of the topics, here are some useful Internet sites. All of them were "live" at the date of publication. Add your own favourite sites and other useful resources.

Animals: www.wwf.org
Energy Sources: www.darvill.clara.net/altenerg
Genetically Modified Organisms: www.nature.ca/genome
Natural Disasters: ndrd.gsfc.nasa.gov
Water: www.oxfam.org.uk/coolplanet
Whales, dolphins and porpoises (cetaceans): www.hwdt.o
Feeding the world: www.fairtrade.org.uk

My environment

Think about your personal environment. Draw some jigsaw puzzle pieces to show the different parts. Show the positive factors, e.g. "clean air" in green, and the dangers, e.g. "lots of traffic", in red.

What is "the environment"?

It contains many different parts, just like the pieces of a big jigsaw puzzle. Human beings, animals, buildings, the earth, the air, the seas, our climate... and all these parts interconnect.

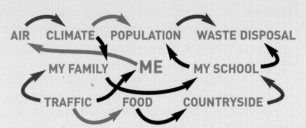

AIR — CLIMATE — POPULATION — WASTE DISPOSAL
MY FAMILY — ME — MY SCHOOL
TRAFFIC — FOOD — COUNTRYSIDE

OXYGEN

If one part of the environment changes, this affects other parts of it, too. Sometimes the changes can be positive. For example, people clean the water in a city. As a result, more oxygen enters the water. Plants grow again, and insects and fish return.

Changes: positive or negative?

Sometimes the changes can be positive *and* negative. For example, there is a lot of traffic in a city. The roads are narrow, and the lorries and cars cannot move. The air is full of traffic fumes. People get ill. The doctors and hospitals are always busy. So the planners decide to build a big road around the city. Traffic can go around it, not through it. The air in the city becomes better - but the new road causes problems, too. The fumes from the traffic pollute the countryside. They affect the fields where farmers grow crops. Animals cannot find their food. One problem goes, and another one appears! We have to think of the results of any changes, now and in the future.

PLANTS

FISH

Our personal environment

The environment is around all of us. We all have a personal environment. This contains our home, our food, our street, all the things that are part of our lives. Each part of it connects with another part. If we want to protect the environment, we must understand these connections. Each part of it affects something else. That's why the environment is so interesting – and so personal.

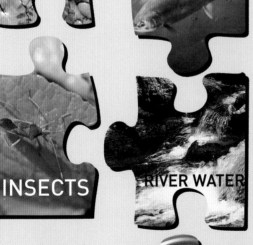

INSECTS

RIVER WATER

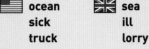

CLEAN WATER

WORD FILE

climate change   The changes that affect our weather.
countryside   The area outside towns and cities.
crops   Farmers grow crops to provide food.
fumes   Smoke or gas from traffic.
global warming   The increase in the earth's temperature.
planner   A person who decides the development of towns.

🇺🇸 ocean	🇬🇧 sea
sick	ill
truck	lorry

3

Using water

Water is a very important part of our environment. But *how* important is it? How many ways do we use water? Here are some of them.

DOMESTIC

Drinking People need to drink clean water every day. Over 1.5 billion people do not have clean drinking water.

Washing Taking a regular shower or a bath is part of our lives. We also use water to wash the dishes, our clothes, and the house. The problem is, this *fresh* water then becomes *waste* water.

Cooking Want to cook some pasta or rice? You need water! Preparing salad? You wash it in water. Boiling potatoes? Water again!

The WHO (World Health Organization) says that a person needs 19 litres of water a day. One in three Asians do not have safe drinking water, and one in two has no sanitation.

AGRICULTURE

Animals Like humans, animals need to drink water to survive.

Irrigation Plants need water, too. So farmers use it to help their crops to grow. With water, dry land can produce crops. When there is no rain, irrigation is necessary for agriculture.

Fish Fish live in fresh water, in lakes and rivers. Many fish live in salt water, in the ocean. These fish are wild, but in many countries there are now also fish farms.

INDUSTRY

Machinery Machines use water.

Transport We transport things by water. Ships travel on the seas, rivers and canals.

Energy Countries where it rains a lot, or with high mountains, use water to produce electricity.

The WHO says that the largest water users are: Agriculture 70%, Industry 20% and Domestic Use 10%.

Over 1.5 billion people do not have clean drinking water.

Keep a Water Diary for a week. Write down all the ways you use water. Estimate how many litres you use.

WORD FILE

crop	The crops in one specific year.
domestic	In the home.
fish farm	A place where fish grow for food.
fresh water	Water with no salt.
irrigation	Watering the land through pipes.
sanitation	Water for toilets.
waste water	Water after we use it.

liter	litre
ocean	sea

Identifying water problems

We all need water. The problem is, there's often too much – or too little. And there are other problems, too. Let's look at some of them.

your town or country. Is there a solution?

PROBLEMS

Quantity	**Too much:** When it rains a lot, the level of the rivers rises. The water runs over the banks. People often drown. Their cars and houses are ruined. Animals drown, too. Many big cities in Asia, Latin America and Europe often have floods. **Too little:** Sometimes it doesn't rain for a long time. Plants die. Animals die, too. People have no food. Many countries in Africa have big problems with droughts. Every year, these droughts get worse and worse.
Pollution	Industry often pollutes water with chemicals. Some farmers also use too many chemicals. These enter the rivers and lakes. They kill the plants and fish.
Politics	Every country wants water for its people. So they build dams to collect it, and to produce hydroelectricity. Sometimes they divert rivers to provide more water. But this often affects other countries. The River Nile is very important for Egypt. The Blue and White Niles rise in Ethiopia and Sudan, in the south. The countries there want to take more of the water before it goes to Egypt. It's not only a problem between one country and another. Different communities *inside* a country need water for different purposes. In Spain, there are plans to build a big dam on the River Ebro to provide irrigation for farmers. But the fishermen at the mouth of the river do not want this. It will destroy the fish and affect *their* lives.
Global warming	The world is getting warmer, so water levels are rising. Climates are changing. Some countries are becoming hotter and drier. This affects agriculture. People want to control global warming, but they cannot agree about the best solutions.

THE RIGHT KIND OF WATER

Every problem has a different solution. That's the interesting challenge – to find the right one! Here's an example of one project.

The place:	Australia.
The problem:	Grapes grow on many hillsides. They need a lot of water. Wine is an important product here. In 2003, the farmers noticed that their plants were dying.
The analysis:	The farmers irrigate their crops, so the water level in the soil is rising. But deep under the whole continent of Australia, there is a lot of salt. The water goes down and the salt comes up! This water in the soil is salty, not fresh. Salt is destroying the grapes, and also Australia's huge wheat crop. Every year, there is less and less salt-free land. By 2050, there will be none.
Finding a solution:	Scientists are trying to develop new kinds of wheat and vines. But will they win the race?

WORD FILE

bank	The high land beside a river.
challenge	A big problem.
dam	A wall across a river or lake.
divert (v)	To change the direction of something.
drown (v)	To go under the water and die.
hydroelectricity	Electricity from water energy.
mouth	The place where a river enters the ocean.
rise (v)	To go up.
salt-free	With no salt.
salt level	The quantity of salt in something.
water level	The height of the water.

The food chain

OK - so everything in the environment is connected (page 3). Let's look at an example. What about a food chain?

Link 1: A food chain begins with a plant. It takes its energy from the sun.
Plants also need water, oxygen and carbon dioxide to grow.
Plants are **producers**: they produce their own energy.

Link 2: Some animals eat plants or seeds to get their energy. Examples of these herbivores are deer, giraffes, zebras, mice and some birds. They are **first-level consumers**.

Link 4: There can be third-level consumers, too! Who eats the snake? Perhaps an eagle. What about the cat? A bigger animal, like a wolf. And the lion? Does anything eat a lion? And what about vultures? They eat a lot of different dead animals. Ugh! But, in fact, this cleans up the environment!

Link 3: Some other animals are carnivores: they eat other animals, such as the **first-level consumers**. Examples are lions (killing and eating a zebra), snakes (eating a mouse), or a cat (eating a bird). These are second-level consumers.

DECOMPOSERS
There are other important organisms in the food chain. Examples are fungi and bacteria. These consume dead plants and animals, and then this food returns to the earth.

WHY ARE FOOD CHAINS IMPORTANT?
They remind us that, if we damage or destroy one link in the chain, this affects the next one. So if humans damage plants, the **producers**, there is no food for the first-level consumers. This can affect the second-level consumers and the third-level consumers, too. The damage to plants can be from natural causes (flood, drought or climate change), or from human causes (pollution or destruction). The result will be the same. Ultimately, there will be no food for humans, either.

Choose a plant or an animal, and work out the links in a food chain for it.

WORD FILE	
climate change	The changes that affect our weather.
consume (v)	To eat something.
damage (v)	To harm something.
destroy (v)	To kill something.
energy	Physical power to do something.
link	A connection.
organism	A living thing.

Humans and the natural world

Watching whales

This began in the U.S. It's now possible to watch whales (and porpoises and dolphins) in lots of other countries, too. It's a great experience to see and identify these huge creatures. Or to watch dolphins as they play games around the boat. You learn a lot, you breathe lots of fresh air – and no one gets hurt. Or do they? Mmm... It's not all good news!

Sound problems

Whales communicate with other whales through sound. However, whale-watchers use boats with noisy engines. So it is difficult for the whales to hear the signals from other whales. They become confused. They cannot send or receive messages about food, or the condition of the ocean.

Pollution

The boats also pollute the water. This can affect plankton and small fish. Plankton? Very, very small plants and animals. Whales are big, but some of them just eat these tiny things. Others eat fish. Boats disturb small fish and plankton, so they destroy the whales' food.

SOLUTIONS!

There is now a code-of-behaviour for whale-watching. Read the full code on the IFAW (International Fund for Animal Welfare) website www.ifaw.org. Here are the main points.

✖ Don't make a sudden noise.
✖ Never chase whales.
✖ Don't disturb mothers and young whales.
✖ Don't pollute the water near whales.

Tourism and whales *can* exist together!

A SPECIAL PROBLEM: Killing whales

In some parts of the world, people like to eat whale meat. So fishermen hunt and kill them. The problem is, the methods are not very efficient – or humane. Most of the meat is in the big fins. So when the men catch a whale, they often cut off the fins. Then they throw the body back into the sea. They can take 20 minutes to die.

Whales are mammals, just like us – imagine if someone cut your arms off and threw you into the sea. Many people who eat whale meat do not know these facts.

Organisations like Greenpeace and IFAW help to protect whales. They work in lots of different countries – and often there are other, national organisations too.

WORD FILE

confused	Not able to think clearly.
fin	The "wings" on the side of a fish.
humane	Kind to animals.
mammal	An animal that drinks its mother's milk as a baby.
tiny	Very, very small.
whale-watcher	A person who watches whales.

🇺🇸 behavior	🇬🇧 behaviour
ocean	sea

Do you know any other codes for human-animal interaction?

ENVIRONMENTAL EYE

Making a difference

The world of whales and dolphins is very interesting. In fact, an organisation in Scotland works with them all the time. They don't only *watch* these creatures, though. They also do research, and they work with humans, too. They organise educational programmes, and they work with the local communities.

What does HWDT do?

1. Research

In this part of the Atlantic Ocean, there are 24 different kinds of whales, porpoises and dolphins (cetaceans). The members of HWDT record where they are, and what they are doing. They do research to understand more about them, and to detect any problems. Is there enough food? Is the water polluted? The scientists also want to see how the cetaceans can co-exist with humans.

This is serious scientific work, and groups of volunteers of all ages help the scientists. Visitors to the HWDT office can use an Observations Sheet to record anything that they see.

This Observations Sheet has descriptions of eight common types of cetaceans. The observers fill in the sheet. They record where they are (e.g. on a boat, on land) and what they can see (description and behaviour of the animal). They also note the number and type (adults or young ones), and the state of the sea and weather.

So hundreds of "ordinary" people can take part in environmental observation and research. It's fun – and it's also important research!

WORD FILE	
cetacean	The family of whales, dolphins and porpoises.
co-exist (v)	To live in the same place.
ferryboat	A boat between two (or more) places.
volunteer	A person who works for no money.

🇺🇸 behavior	🇬🇧 behaviour
organize	organise

2. Educational projects

The HWDT scientists have a sailing boat, the "Silurian". For ten days every month, they use this boat for research. But for the rest of the month, the boat becomes a "floating classroom". The Education team visit the schools on all the islands, and primary and secondary students come on board. In this way, they learn about the sea environment in a practical way. Science, maths, computer studies and geography all become *real*!

SCHOOLS
The team also do lessons in the schools on land. They want to introduce the students to different kinds of cetaceans. How can they do this? They can't take a live animal into the classroom – but they *can* take a life-size model!

Minke whales are the most common kind here. They are about nine metres long. When the students see the model in their classroom, those measurements become real! They can compare the length of the whale with their own height.

Whales are mammals. How do they breathe? The students can touch the two blowholes and understand this. They can also see how they eat. Do they have teeth?

Well, what *does* this huge animal eat? Plankton! What's that? Very, very small plants and animals. A big minke whale eats a lot of plankton every day. So if the water is polluted and there's no plankton, the whale starves. It has to move to a new part of the ocean.

PROJECTS

The students do projects, too. For example, they read the computer data and compare results from two different years. They analyse the differences, and suggest reasons. This is *real* science!

They also experiment with dolphin communication. They often do an activity in pairs. They close their eyes, and try to find their partner, using special sounds (clicks and whistles) just like dolphins and whales. It's very dark under the sea, so communicating through sound is really important. (See page 7 for more about this.)

In this way, the students connect the environment with maths, science and IT.

WORD FILE

analyse (v)	To study something in detail.
blowhole	A hole in a whale or dolphin's head; it breathes through this.
enthusiastic	Very interested in something.
IT	Information technology.
life-size	The same size as the real thing.
model	A copy of something.
screen	The "window" of a computer.
species	A family of animals.
starve (v)	To have no food so that you can die.

🇺🇸 analyze	🇬🇧 analyse
math	maths
meter	metre
ocean	sea

OPEN DOOR

The HWDT office in Tobermory is a great place to visit.
There are photographs, fact-sheets and computers. For example, every species of whale or dolphin makes a different sound. You can click onto a screen, and listen to these sounds. Most important of all, there are enthusiastic people to talk to!

What other school subjects can you link with the environment?
Can you think of any songs, or music, or literature connections?

ENVIRONMENTAL EYE

Feeding the world

The environment is about plants and animals – but it's about humans, too. They need to work and earn money, and they also need to eat. Many people do not have enough food. So scientists and governments are always looking for new ways to feed them. The problem is, many of these new discoveries and ideas bring new problems!

1. GM crops: solution or problem?

Supermarkets want to sell cheap food – and fruit and vegetables that look big and bright and "perfect". To grow these, some farmers use more and more chemicals on their crops. When you eat an apple, do you know what chemicals are on the skin? What is the effect of these on our health?

GM (Genetically-modified) crops sound like a great idea. They don't get diseases like normal crops. They produce lots of strong plants. They are cheap. Isn't this a great way to feed the world, especially poor countries?

The problem is, nobody knows the consequences! Will these crops affect human health? What happens if something goes wrong? Can GM crops encourage diseases like cancer? Nobody knows for certain! So people are nervous.

Are GM crops a step too far? Will they affect our environment – and us? We don't know!

WORD FILE

benefit (v)	To get something good from a situation.
care (v)	To feel responsible for people.
consumer	A person who buys things.
contribute (v)	To give something.
degenerate (v)	To get worse.
fair	Equal for everybody.
guarantee (v)	To make sure that something happens.
hurricane	A very strong wind.
movement	A group of people with the same ideas.
sugar cane	Farmers grow this plant to produce sugar.
supply chain	The series of processes to move food from the origin to the consumer.

🇺🇸 cookies		🇬🇧 biscuits	
organize		organise	
publicize		publicise	

2. Fairtrade

Look at the logo on these products.

FAIRTRADE

In many countries, farmers have to sell their fruit and vegetables for very low prices. If they increase these prices, supermarkets will not buy them. There are other problems, too. When there is a drought, or a flood, farmers often lose their crops. Then they have no money.

In 1994, a new organisation, Fairtrade, decided to help farmers. Their motto is "A fair price for good food". This organization works with both farmers and supermarkets, the different parts of the supply chain. They guarantee a good price to the farmers, and they contribute money to educational and social projects. The supermarkets sell the products at a higher price, but it's a fair one. And the consumer gets good quality, at a fair price. Everyone in this supply chain benefits!

In 2004, Fairtrade worked with similar organisations in 17 other countries in Europe, North America and Asia. There are more and more countries every year. There are now more than 130 products with the Fairtrade logo. These include coffee, tea, chocolate, bananas, fruit juice, sugar and honey. The products come from more than 40 countries.

> "We are indebted to half the world before we finish breakfast."
> Martin Luther King

Who benefits?

1. The environment: fewer chemicals and better farming methods.
2. The suppliers: guaranteed income and money for social projects.
3. The supermarkets: guaranteed quality and supply.
4. The consumer: good quality, and the opportunity to help poorer people in other countries.

So the whole global environment benefits.

The growers

Carlos is a farmer in Cuba. He grows oranges. His father and grandfather were farmers, too. They grew sugar cane. He is part of a group of 70 orange farmers. They meet every day for meals, and for social activities. Fairtrade guarantees a good price for the oranges. They are using some of this money to build better houses. In Cuba, there are often hurricanes. These damage houses and the orange trees. Carlos says, "With Fairtrade, we have the opportunity to spend money on houses for the cooperative farmers and something for recreation".

Ana and Jose are farmers in Ecuador. They grow bananas. "We don't use many chemicals - Fairtrade limits this. Some companies don't care. Chemicals make the fruit grow quickly at first. But then they enter the soil, and it degenerates. But we need the Fairtrade price to support us."

The consumers: getting involved

Some places in the U.K. are now "Fairtrade Towns". They use Fairtrade products in schools, hospitals and public places. The supermarkets and food stores sell them. Some schools organise events to publicise the organisation. They have fashion shows and world music concerts.

There are even some Fairtrade universities. After all, students drink lots of coffee, tea and juice. They like to eat chocolate and biscuits. So now they can support the environment and poorer countries at the same time. This is now a popular movement among students.

The countries and products (2004)		
Coffee	**Cocoa**	**Honey**
Cameroon	Belize	Chile
Colombia	Bolivia	Mexico
Costa Rica	Dominican	Uruguay
Dominican	Republic	**Sugar**
Republic	**Fresh fruits and juices**	Malawi
Guatemala	Brazil	Paraguay
Haiti	Colombia	**Tea**
Indonesia	Costa Rica	India
Mexico	Dominican	Sri Lanka
Nicaragua	Republic	Tanzania
Papua New Guinea	Ecuador	Uganda
Peru	Ghana	Kenya
Rwanda	South Africa	**Vegetables**
		Egypt

What do you eat for breakfast? Where do the things come from? Who grows them? Who makes them? What can you find out about the food supply chain for each item?

ENVIRONMENTAL EYE

Energy: where the wind blows

Wind can provide energy. In the past, sailors used the wind for their sailing ships. Farmers used it to grind corn, in windmills. Now the modern world needs a lot of energy. We use electricity to heat our houses, for computers, for transport. Where will it come from in the future? Many people wonder if wind farms are the solution.

Based on information provided by WWF - Scotland.

What is a wind farm?

In some places, there are groups of 20 or 30 wind machines. These enormous windmills produce electricity. They stand on hillsides, in windy places. In some of these places, the wind can be more than 100 kilometres an hour. Some of the wind machines are 90 metres high. They can produce a lot of electricity! Sounds good, doesn't it?

The school wind machine

There's a lot of wind in the north of Scotland. One of the schools decided to have its own wind machine. The WWF (World Wildlife Fund) and the government gave them some money. Now their machine provides their electricity. It does other things, too. The students use it in maths lessons. They calculate how much money they are saving with this free energy. They watch the dials, and realise that the school never stops using power. Fridges and heating systems need electricity even at the weekends and in the holidays. The students see that they can save energy if they turn off lights and computers.

The machine has a name: Dragonfly.

Wind farms

It's not all good news. There is a new plan to build a lot of wind farms around the coasts of Britain. But a lot of people are against this. They think the environment will suffer.

For example, what about the migratory birds that fly to and from Britain every year? Big birds like swans and geese fly at about 40 metres above the sea. They won't see the machines, and they'll fly into them. Then there's the noise. For people who live near these "monsters", this is terrible. In fact, in today's environment, noise pollution is a real problem.

The discussion "for and against" wind farms is still continuing. But for the students at Lunnasting Primary School in Shetland, their Dragonfly is a big "plus".

WORD FILE

dial	A round instrument that shows quantity.
"for and against"	The two sides of a problem.
grind (v)	To break something into very small pieces or powder.
heating system	The machines to make a building warm.
migratory	Going to a warmer or colder part of the world.
monster	A large, frightening imaginary creature.
"pluses and minuses"	The positive and negative points.
windmill	A machine that uses wind to produce energy.

🇺🇸	🇬🇧
kilometer	kilometre
math	maths
meter	metre
realize	realise
vacations	holidays

Find out about other forms of alternative energy, such as solar power from the sun, or fuel for cars from alcohol. Check out the "pluses and minuses".

ENVIRONMENT

NATURAL  DISASTERS

Scientists understand a lot about the environment – but they don't understand everything! Every year, there are big and small disasters in different parts of the world. Some of these happen very often, but some of them are a big shock. How do these natural disasters affect humans? Can we do anything about them?

 What natural disasters can occur in your country? When and where was the last one?

HURRICANES

WHAT are they?

✗ Tropical storms with strong winds. They start at sea, and can travel a long distance. They have different names in different places: "hurricanes" in the Atlantic Ocean, "typhoons" in the Pacific Ocean, "tropical cyclones" in the Indian Ocean and around Australasia.

✗ Tornadoes, or whirlwinds, are similar, but begin over land.

WHY do they happen?

✗ The water evaporates from the warm sea. This condenses in the atmosphere. More and more hot, wet air rises up. It becomes a strong wind.

WHERE do they happen?

✗ Over the warm parts of oceans. Tornadoes are common in parts of the U.S.A., Australia, and Japan.

HOW do they affect people?

✗ They can affect ships, blow down houses, cause floods and disrupt traffic.

WHAT can people do?

✗ Scientists can usually track hurricanes, but they cannot stop them.

FLOODS

WHAT are they?

✗ The water in rivers, lakes or the ocean rises above its normal level and goes onto the land.

WHY do they happen?

✗ If there is a lot of rain, or very strong winds, floods can happen.

WHERE do they happen?

✗ Some rivers in Bangladesh and India flood every year.

✗ People expect it, so there is no panic. When the floods go down, there are lots of minerals in the soil. They can grow good plants.

HOW do they affect people?

✗ When the floods are a surprise, many people can drown.

✗ Every year, people lose their houses and their furniture.

✗ When floods happen every year, some people are ready for them. But many people (and governments) do not prepare properly.

WHAT can people do?

✗ Dams can reduce floods – but some dams can *cause* them! There are often "flood warnings" on the radio.

WORD FILE

dam	A wall across a river or lake.
disaster	A very bad event.
disrupt (v)	To interrupt something.
drown (v)	To go under the water and die.
evaporate (v)	To change into gas.
shock	A very big surprise.

🇺🇸 ocean   🇬🇧 sea

Do you know?

(Answers on page 16.)

1. WORD BOX

Use the clues and unjumble the words.
All the words are in this Portfolio.

W	Z	P	T	W	C	N	E	S	G	P
Y	K	F	U	T	U	R	E	L	Q	V
C	L	L	F	G	A	S	A	O	R	B
B	X	O	I	E	N	E	R	G	Y	T
R	D	O	U	K	H	N	T	C	I	D
B	J	D	R	O	U	G	H	T	Y	M
U	T	V	Z	Y	W	M	Q	A	I	O
G	S	S	B	X	A	L	U	F	X	R
I	H	U	R	R	I	C	A	N	E	V
G	D	T	F	R	W	C	K	X	P	T
M	P	R	O	D	U	C	E	R	S	N
C	J	D	R	A	P	R	Y	G	R	E

Across
1. Looking ahead into the TERUFU.
2. Wind and the sun give us RENEGY.
3. When there is not enough rain, there's a GROTDUH.
4. Every ENACHRIRU has a name.
5. Consumers eat CEUPORD.

Down
1. A little water is good, but too much produces a LOFOD.
2. In Japan, they build special houses because they have a lot of ARTEKEQUAHs.

2. PLACES

Can you link these geographical features and places?

a. Plate   ☐ desert
b. Korea   ☐ mountain
c. Pacific   ☐ river
d. Grand   ☐ plain
e. Sahara   ☐ lake
f. Serengeti   ☐ volcano
g. Tasmania   ☐ canyon
h. Everest   ☐ island
i. Etna   ☐ ocean
j. Titicaca   ☐ peninsula

3. CONTINENTS

Now put the places in 2 on the map in the right continents. Draw a symbol and write the name. WARNING! One place is not in a continent!

Projects

Environmental Study

Choose an area in your town.
Study it for a week.
Find out about its history,
its problems, the good
things about it.
Present these to your friends.

1

Fast Food x Slow Food

Find a recipe for making a milk shake, or
ice cream. List the ingredients. Now find
the same product in a supermarket.
Look at the label. List the contents.
How many chemicals
are there in the list?

2

Animal Protection T-Shirt

What's your favourite wild animal? How can
we protect it? Make up a slogan and
design a T-shirt for your animal.
If possible, have an Environmental
Fashion Show with your friends.

3

Protect Our Environment!

Choose something in your
environment that needs protecting.
What's the problem?
Is there a solution? What?
Who can help? Design a poster
to advertise your campaign.
Use photos, drawings, slogans.

4

A Seasons Diary

Choose a season: Spring, Summer,
Fall/Autumn, or Winter. What is going to
happen? What does happen? Keep an
environmental diary. Write your predictions.
Then write the reality! Use these items:

✖ PLANTS
✖ ANIMALS
✖ BIRDS
✖ TEMPERATURE
✖ WEATHER
✖ OTHER

5

Research Project

Choose a plant, animal or piece of nature
(river, park, etc.). Find out everything
you can about it. Use this information
to write part of an Environmental Tourist
Guide. Use photos, interview, texts,
drawings... Anything!

6

**Collect your Environmental Eye projects.
Select the best ones, and make an
Environmental Exhibition.**

Topics chatrooms

Teens chat

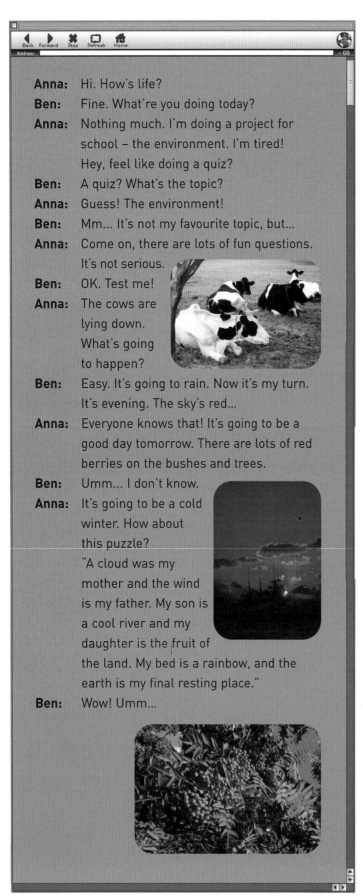

Anna: Hi. How's life?

Ben: Fine. What're you doing today?

Anna: Nothing much. I'm doing a project for school – the environment. I'm tired! Hey, feel like doing a quiz?

Ben: A quiz? What's the topic?

Anna: Guess! The environment!

Ben: Mm... It's not my favourite topic, but...

Anna: Come on, there are lots of fun questions. It's not serious.

Ben: OK. Test me!

Anna: The cows are lying down. What's going to happen?

Ben: Easy. It's going to rain. Now it's my turn. It's evening. The sky's red...

Anna: Everyone knows that! It's going to be a good day tomorrow. There are lots of red berries on the bushes and trees.

Ben: Umm... I don't know.

Anna: It's going to be a cold winter. How about this puzzle?

"A cloud was my mother and the wind is my father. My son is a cool river and my daughter is the fruit of the land. My bed is a rainbow, and the earth is my final resting place."

Ben: Wow! Umm...

The answer's in the Facts Check (don't cheat!).

Can you believe it?

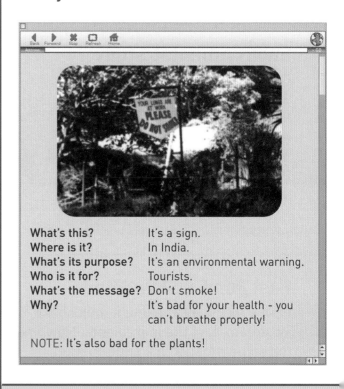

What's this?   It's a sign.
Where is it?   In India.
What's its purpose?   It's an environmental warning.
Who is it for?   Tourists.
What's the message?   Don't smoke!
Why?   It's bad for your health – you can't breathe properly!

NOTE: It's also bad for the plants!

Facts Check

Page 14   **1. WORD BOX**
Across: FUTURE/ENERGY/DROUGHT/ HURRICANE/PRODUCERS
Down: FLOOD/EARTHQUAKE

2. PLACES
a. river; b. peninsula; c. ocean; d. canyon; e. desert; f. plain; g. island; h. mountain; i. volcano; j. lake

3. CONTINENTS
AFRICA: Sahara / Serengeti
AMERICAS: Plate / Titicaca / Grand Canyon
ASIA: Everest; Korea
AUSTRALASIA: Tasmania
EUROPE: Etna
other: Pacific

Page 16   **TEENS CHAT:** rain

Goodbye!
Well, that's the end of 'Environment'. We hope you'll continue with your Environmental Eye work. See you in the next Topics title.
Bye for now!

Susan Holden